MW01712130

Cloud Therapy

a book about swimming

drawing by Norton Wisdom

Cloud Therapy

a book about swimming

Jason Weiss

for Jo—
with love,
Jason
8 Oct. 15

Talisman House, Publishers
Northfield, Massachusetts•2015

Published in the United States of America by
Talisman House, Publishers
P.O. Box 102
Northfield, Massachusetts 01360

11 12 13 7 6 5 4 3 2 1 First Edition

Manufactured in the United Sates of America
Printed on acid-free paper

ISBN: 978-1-58498-116-9

frontispiece by Norton Wisdom
reproduced by permission of the artist

cover, detail from Thomas Eakins,
"The Swimming Hole" (1884-85), oil on canvas,
Amon Carter Museum, Fort Worth, Texas.

for Morris S. Weiss, 1924-2015,
lifelong swimmer

What are the great measurements of time, of distance, but tools with which to imagine our own experience? As a child, I knew that we lived an hour and a half from New York City, sixty miles: a couple of TV shows, perhaps the length of a baseball game. Later, as a teenager in California, I knew that we were half an hour from San Francisco, and yet an hour's flight from L. A. Driving in the Bay Area of the 1970s, that was a mere fifteen miles over local roads, the freeway, the Bay Bridge; though, from airport to airport, some four hundred miles. Later still, in my footloose Paris years, I came to consider practically every distance I covered in the city from one point to another, whether on foot or by metro or bus, as taking half an hour. Of course, I was often late, and even sometimes early. But, as ever, distance was measured above all by time; accurately or not, it was the experience of moving through that distance, whatever the means of my locomotion.

Living in Brooklyn these twenty-plus years now, I figure that in my lifetime I have swum the equivalent of from here to Salt Lake City. What does that mean? I first took up swimming as a discipline early in 1985—or was it the end of the previous year?—at the age of 29. By the summer, I had managed to work my way up to swimming a mile without stop, doing the crawl. There I have remained ever since, occasionally swimming further, depending on the circumstance, but as a general rule I thought a mile was enough. Nor was I ever concerned about speed. Far as I was concerned, past attaining a certain reasonable pace, speed was completely pointless. Eventually, I reached a time of about forty minutes to the mile; it felt as natural as my particular walking pace, when left to my own devices. And that was one of the great discoveries about swimming for me, self-evident though it may be: by the very nature of the medium you had only your own devices, and I liked that simplicity.

Swimming is a constant measure, like a metronome, internally generated, conditioned by the elements of water, body, air. It is also a measuring without end, spinning out figures, ratios, relationships in changing perspectives. First and most immediate, the language of numbers asserts its ineffable domain in a continuous shifting of values: distance covered, distance remaining, in absolute numbers, fractions, inversions of terms, modular frequencies, comparative velocities, in and out of phase.

I have swum in pools of different lengths, where the magic number of how many laps to the mile totaled forty-eight, sixty-four, seventy-two, even thirty-two. When I say laps, I'm counting them in one direction, what at least one lifeguard insists are really lengths; a lap, he says, is there and back, round trip, and that makes sense, but nonetheless I cling to my use of the word. And habituated as I am to swimming pools, to the chlorine scrubbing in and out my body, its detergent smell on my arms later in the day, when I've swum in ponds and across inlets of the sea, curiously, I can only measure distance by the time it takes me to swim a certain path—an unreliable calculation, to be sure, though aided by certain estimates of a roughly parallel route along the shore.

The numbers games, for me, are among the necessary and inevitable amusements while my head goes soaring through the water for the span of those forty minutes. Four laps down: not just sixty-eight more to go, nearly an untenable number, but also one-eighteenth gone, which is still to say a long way yet to go, while cranking up the growing spin of numbers. Thus, rounding the turn from eight laps entering into the ninth is also to mark a larger advance, from one-ninth to one-eighth of a mile, and soon almost one-seventh. The play of fractions accelerates from there, while the proximity of denominators expands and contracts almost with every turn. At twenty-four laps, that's one-third of the distance covered, a few minutes since reaching a quarter-mile and more than six minutes before the three collapses to two for a half-mile, but in between there is twenty-seven, three-eighths, which not only begins to sound substantial but also rings one of those bells of other values. Since I swim a mile in forty minutes, and the pool in question is seventy-two laps, that makes nine laps every five minutes, and so twenty-seven (laps) is also fifteen (minutes). And there is a further set of nodal points that have their own resonance: since I first took to swimming as a regular discipline while living in Paris, I also took on the habit of thinking in kilometers, so that forty-five laps (what remains to swim after those twenty-seven) also rings in my head as a kilometer. It's another measure of distance that plays quietly under the surface, like an alternate alphabet.

But how is it that numbers can have any relation to water? At least in a swimming pool, they seem to mold each other into the same mixed medium, bound by the hard edges of the basin that contains them, that lends bounce to their constant play. Just as the water sloshes about there starting with the first human body plying its orderly or disorderly path, so the numbers unseen jostle and slosh and change places constantly, in their hapless and slippery perspectives of measurement—of merriment too, perhaps, though that may be one of our special attachments to numbers, the idea that they are without emotion, hence no merriment or melancholy either. Yet I have never quite understood: are numbers man-made or simply discovered as a language of deep structure to the world, regardless of the human presence? If man-made or at least conceptualized by the human mind, do numbers then carry some trace of the emotional stamp that marks the curious creatures that we are? I suppose, giddy or garrulous, so many numbers roiling about with their boisterous party in the pool might leave no room for us swimmers. Then again, numbers are abstract, are they not, whereas water, of course, is—well, not concrete, but tangible, sort of. The length of a pool, not just for swimmers but for the water that fills it as well, represents a unit, a singular instance before an implied repetition. That singular instance, for the swimmer, is multiplied however many times a person decides, by will or weariness, its oneness unfolding and unfolding again. As for the water, any containment is always provisional, ever challenging the very instinct to measure, for its own inclination in the long run is to join with the wide immeasurable sea.

THIS MORNING, SWIMMING MY LAPS, a song floated into consciousness. "I'd love to get you on a slow boat to China / all to myself, alone . . . " What it was doing there, why that song and not another, I have no idea. As though borrowed from a dream somewhere, or from a particular scene in a play or movie that I saw in the recent past; I could almost picture it, the ironic tone, the moonlit reverie. Not so often do specific tunes enter my thoughts while swimming, but when they do I think in large part they sail in on a rhythm. I cannot say if I swim in 4/4 time, only that it is steady, regular, constant—like walking, like breathing—as if an echo of my heartbeat. That corresponds as well to my sense of the general experience when I swim, no matter how often I've managed to do so at any given period: when I set forth in the water, I put my body on automatic pilot and let my mind wander. It doesn't matter if I'm sharing the lane with other swimmers; I see them ahead or behind, they hardly affect my pace. That steady rhythm of my limbs, my breathing, not overly fast nor slow, would seem to underlie most any song. Yet it is only a certain tone of thought, of memory or mood or atmosphere, that mysteriously calls forth a specific song while I swim—and even then it may soon fade away, or linger stubbornly, past all reason. When walking along the street, I often take to whistling a tune made up on the spot to match my steps, or I'll start with a familiar tune and soon veer off, but the frequency of such tunefulness, though propelled by my own internal mechanical rhythms, does not arise quite so much when my head is in the water. As if air were a crucial element in that peculiar alchemy. I once made an experiment in that regard, which I have at moments repeated: while I swam, I tried to hum a certain melody. I think it may have been one of those great emboldening melodies played by the South African jazz groups that I love, as if the music could grant me renewed strength and I might swim many miles. Right away, it became clear that I could not hum with my head in the water and keep up my usual rhythm of breathing. That humming, with its small way of projecting sound out beyond my head, required precious oxygen. Which meant, less for me as I swam. I had thought that tuneful buzzing, the humble vibration into sound emanating from the closed mouth, might be produced irrespective of inhaling or exhaling. But that was just as well: imagine a pool, a pond, a sea full of swimmers humming away, the cacophony!

MY TRAJECTORY TO THE POINT OF TAKING UP swimming as a regular practice was a curious one—curious to me, at least, in its necessary detours of resistance. I had grown up across the street from the beach, at the Jersey shore, and we belonged to the big private beach club in town, also across the street. The Deal Casino had a large swimming pool, rows and rows of cabanas that families rented for the season, among which the wives played mahjong and the men their card games, as well as a snack bar, shuffleboard courts, ping pong tables, and the beach itself which was fenced off from the public beach next door at Phillips Avenue. I used to play shuffleboard sometimes, especially with Junior Lister who was older than my own folks, and though I seldom would just lie in the sand roasting like a piece of meat, I did go body surfing and otherwise play in the water, but rarely (never?) did I get in the pool and swim as if it were, you know, exercise. I loved to jump off the diving board where I would practice front and back somersaults, half and full gainers, once or twice even hitting my foot on the board. The idea of exercise, for me as a kid, was not attractive: it would only happen if I didn't have to think that's what I was doing—playing baseball, riding my bicycle—and so, even across the street from the beach, on a hot day swimming was more about getting wet, frolicking in the water. Perhaps the equivalent of piano lessons, for years in summer and winter I was carted off for swimming lessons. Not just so that I would learn how to, and never ever forget, but that I would actually continue to swim.

For a few years in the early 1980s, in the latter half of my bohemian twenties, I lived with a woman in Paris who was older than me, who had a history of bodily ailments and so, for longer than I knew her, had taken to easing her pains with a regimen of swimming in public pools. Of course, exercise as a purpose, a desired activity, was still anathema to me. I loved to walk long distances in the city, covering ground in great strides as if I could take in everything; I always felt that, were I somehow to find myself day or night without a cent, I could easily cross the city on foot, such was my sense of the dimensions of Paris with respect to my own physical capacities and the pleasure of moving through its streets. But for the sake of exercise? That wasn't the point. Besides, we lived in a small one-bedroom apartment, converted from two maid's rooms, six flights up from the street. With mail delivery three times a day back then, I thought nothing of dashing down and up those hundred and two steps just to see if anything had come for me; it was not unusual for me to climb those stairs five times a day. So, in spite of my essentially sedentary ways as a writer and reader, I never thought of exercise as something to go out and actually do.

Then, one winter, I came back from an extended stay in Spain with a bout of hepatitis from bad shellfish. Clearly, Jews of old knew something I didn't know. Like a good doctor's son, I had managed to be almost completely ignorant of any medical condition that hadn't touched me directly, but such was the overwhelming evidence of my symptoms that something was not right in my body, that within a day or two of my return to Paris I strolled across the Jardin des Plantes from where I lived on the Rue Monge, which let me out across from the Gare d'Austerlitz train station. Just down the block from the station was the public hospital Salpêtrière (only now do I wonder by what logic the city planners once thought it a good idea to locate a major hospital complex beside an important train route: the hospital came first, originally the site of a gunpowder factory, and both are by the river). I found my way to the building with the clinic, waited an hour for my turn, and when I recounted my symptoms to the doctor, he leaned back with a triumphant grin and announced, "Why, you have hepatitis!" That sounded serious; I nearly fainted. The nurse, cigarette in one hand (this was 1984), took my blood and said to call next week for the results.

Despite the newfound appreciation of my own mortality, it was not until late that year somehow, around when I turned 29, that it occurred to me I might, I should, I could do something for the benefit of my physical well-being, something regular and sufficiently rigorous, something that others (not me) might even call exercise. Thanks no doubt to the example of that older girlfriend who had at last moved out in the spring (some six or eight months after I had encouraged her to do so—life is complicated, as is housing), and certainly thanks to my parents who all through my childhood made me take lessons, the only physical discipline that even presented itself to my mind as a denizen of that city, short of outright *libertinage* (which I was not necessarily against in principle, but way too much bother), was swimming. And Paris, as it happens, was a marvel when it comes to municipal services like providing its citizens with public pools. And I mean pools the size in which one can swim laps—two or three in each arrondissement, something like fifty pools throughout the entire city (and if I exaggerate, it is not by terribly much; even if the number were half that, it would be impressive as a measure of public amenities). Over the next four-plus years, I swam in seven or eight of those many pools in Paris. However, the concept of swimming laps, in most of the pools, was practiced by a minority contingent.

My first day at the pool on the Rue de Pontoise. What was I doing there? Everyone seemed to belong—by the simple fact that they were already there—but me. A block from the river, off the Boulevard St. Germain, just east of the Place Maubert, the building dated from the 1930s, I would guess—possibly the oldest of the pools I frequented. Though I could glimpse the pool with its tiled walls beyond the partition where I paid my fee at the front desk, I proceeded upstairs as instructed to the changing booths which were arrayed all along a balcony overlooking the pool. The attendant led me to an empty booth, and minutes later I was standing by the pool ready for action. But knowing how to swim was one thing; submitting myself to the chaos and cacophony before me was quite another. At first glance, I saw no order at all among the several dozen bathers. (And what were they all doing there in the middle of the day? Were they all nominal bohemians like me?) People of all ages dove in, jumped in, from the sides, the ends, the corners, splashing about or plunging halfway across before stopping and changing direction, oblivious to possible collisions. And yet, in the midst of all that random turbulence, I noticed a woman calmly plying through the waters from one end of the pool to the other and back again. How was it possible? I became aware of a couple of others carving a straight path as well, but the woman made it seem effortless. It dawned on me that swimming laps was a nice idea, but maybe not so easy?

Shedding whatever last excuses I could still muster, I climbed into the pool and pushed off. Avoiding any number of unidentified splashing objects veering toward me from the sides, I found that the biggest challenge was just to keep breathing as I propelled myself forward, swim and breathe, and to do both in a regular way until I reached the other end. By the time I did get to the other end, I was exhausted! Gripping the side while I caught my breath, I glanced about: did no one notice my achievement? Incredible as it seemed, I had to accept that my efforts were less than insignificant to others around me. But as I rested there contemplating how does one get from here to there and back again, and again and again, with no more strain than a pendulum, I decided to attempt the impossible and return the way I came. Heedless of the dangers, I set out–yet, despite my most valiant intentions, I had to abandon the quest. Just where my feet could reach the bottom, I touched down and walked the rest of the way, as if I'd washed ashore. Determined I was, though, to try again the next day.

I'm talking here about the crawl, freestyle, stick your face in the water and lift it out again a little further to take another breath. The other strokes I never took seriously, not since I began swimming laps. Breast stroke, what was that but locomotion by default, as a means of not sinking, and because of the forward movement providing the illusion of exercise. Back stroke, which I had always been pretty good at, posed its own problems in a public pool, such as not easily seeing where you were going, but also it canceled the centrality of a key element to the discipline, the control of breathing. As for the butterfly, who in their right mind could justify using that obnoxious stroke in a shared space? Like practicing the drums while your roommate is studying, or launching into your full aerobics routine in the middle of a communal kitchen. Clearly none of those were for me. Was I a Jacobin of swimming? But if I was ever to advance in my ability toward the effortless gliding back and forth as displayed by the woman in the pool that day, I had a lot of work ahead of me.

The next day, I managed to swim from one end of the pool to the other and back again without stopping. I thought I was going to explode. And when I arrived back to where I'd started, still no applause, no recognition. I didn't find that woman there to marvel at, but a few others were cutting through the waters in their less than elegant manners, far more adept than I. And at last, I plunged forth to eke out another round trip amid the tohu-bohu of gratuitous splashers. Having doubled the previous day's plateau, I took a well-deserved rest and studied the other swimmers, to see if I could discern some order that had so far escaped me. I concluded soon enough that a public pool in France was not a place for order or reason, except in the matter of closing time. Taking one last couple of unhurried laps–breaststroke–to better survey the scene and in this way prolong my adaptation to the new element of water, I thought surely I could go further the next day.

And so it was, I advanced by increments. By some strange determination, I quickly made a habit of going to the pool, four times a week or so. The next day, I climbed a different rung, trading quantity for endurance: there and back, and there and back again. Even if these small accomplishments were strictly my own affair, that did not stop me from basking in some measure of satisfaction. The truth was, I didn't know how I did it–to think that only two days earlier I could barely swim to the other end without feeling completely winded! Had I tapped into some secret rhythm? The few swimmers doing laps, each time different than the last, maintained a certain evenness, a constancy and economy of motion, albeit not so gracefully as the woman of the first day. Just as water, over time, and through its own ceaseless motion, inevitably polishes stones, so the regular application of the swimmer's body to his or her task must gradually make for smoother movements. Nice theory, at least; I can't say it's necessarily been proven by some swimmers I've seen over the years. By the end of that first week, I had made it to eight laps, most of them continuous. Thus I was embarked on the perpetual play of numbers, not just as a means to reach further, but also by fractions and ratios as a method to compare what was hypothetically left. Why I latched onto the marker, early on, of a mile, I'm not sure, just that it seemed about right. The pool at the Rue de Pontoise was thirty-three meters in length, and so forty-eight laps made a mile (which I later rounded up to fifty). Therefore, one-sixth of a mile was my high point for the week, and that sounded not half-bad in those terms. By my second week, I was sure to reach a quarter-mile.

PUSHING OFF THE SIDE OF THE POOL, at the beginning of my swim and with each new lap, I'm filled with a strange sensation of flying. Soaring along at the surface of the water, gazing down at the tiled floor, I have often thought how nice it might be if the bottom were painted. Specifically, as a reader in childhood of superhero comic books, most of all Superman, I would love to look down at the tops of buildings as I flew past high above. I once suggested as much to the regular lifeguard at the pool in Grand Army Plaza where I've gone for years now. His sensible rejoinder: that might be scary, it could make people nervous, scared of heights with such a view. Still, I think it would be fun.

Visual real estate like that for a captive audience of swimmers is ripe with wonderful possibilities; though I can also imagine the opportunity taken to complete ruination. When will we see the first corporate logo, the first billboard, at the bottom of a pool where previous sources of funding prove insufficient? But I would like to fly above not just cityscapes like an aquatic man of steel, but also mountains and prairies, coastlines, and why not, even planets! Could that not be a new domain for video projection (although a moving image at the bottom of a pool might indeed be destabilizing)? At which point, why not project the sea floor itself?

Think of the collisions among swimmers! And the aquatic film clubs, theoreticians, trivia compilers. What is certain, at any rate, is that the visual element is paramount in swimming and yet almost taken for granted. Corresponding to that sensation of flying when I push off from the side, I notice how other people enter the pool and how they push off as well. To extend the comic book resonance, when particular swimmers propel themselves forcefully from the sides (I notice this more in approaching as they are leaving), the bubbles streaming behind them, the jets of motion etched in the water, appear much like the vapor and currents of air that trail behind superheroes as they fly, or at least when they are first setting forth through the air. By what laws of force and waves and motion did the cartoonists make the effects in air appear much as in water? In a similar way, occasionally a swimmer will jump into the deep end plunging straight down like a rocket, momentarily lost in the column of bubbles in his wake, before he surfaces again and pushes forth across the pool. That may well be another small delight reaching back to the playful roots of childhood.

FROM EARLY ON IN THAT INTERMITTENT LIFE—like a dream world that we return to with anticipation and abandon, as if it were but a subrhythm within our waking life (or what we think of as our waking life, in which we leave some kind of wake behind us, though seldom quite what we imagine)—once I was able to get beyond the exclusive concentration on my own efforts, one of my favorite amusements came to be watching the bodies of my fellow swimmers. Unlike fish (I think), we don't actively communicate under water, but we do see and look at others around us. I do, at least. How the bodies are shaped—thin or round, taut or lumpy—and how those bodies move. The cut and color of the bathing suit also add to the spectacle, and provoke idle wondering about just why the person chose that shiny or drab pattern, maybe it's time to buy a new suit, this one's not so flattering. My thoughts do not arrive at many conclusions about the personality or habits of other swimmers, at least not based on their suits or the shapes of their bodies; rather, such sights draw my attention along for a little while before it wanders off. But there are times when a particularly shapely body (usually female, but not always) sustains my curiosity enough to imagine what must the face look like, floating along there on the surface of the water. Or more likely to question, for my mind does not go so far as to pull up an image of a face. I'm speaking of swimmers I haven't seen before, or noticed in that way, but it is always an elusive puzzle: inevitably there is some measure of surprise to discover that face, almost disappointment even, to find the face less attractive than expected for such a figure, or older, or younger. And in each instance that surprise is also a bit disturbing, to realize my interest was drawn by someone so young, or so old, or that the dull face on that shapely body should prove disappointing, as if to suggest that I'm not above such crass sentiments, after all. For while these observations of bodies are not exactly sexual, it is hardly an accident that those bodies and not others attract my notice.

It is nearly the inverse experience on dry land, away from the water. Seeing those same swimmers in their street clothes, their hair combed, without swim caps and goggles, as if we'd all been transformed into earthlings again (but had this other existence in common), inevitably brings its own surprise, as we recognize each other uncertainly at first. But also that unsettling separation of face and body in the water, especially when experienced from under the water, plays out in much the opposite way in our normal life. Most often, our bodies are far more covered by clothes, more concealed than any swimsuit could do, so that it is again like they are under water or separated, nearly hidden from view, in comparison to what's on top. While we perceive the general shape of the bodies around us on the street, it is the faces that draw us in. The eyes, the gaze, the mouth; the expressions and gestures; perhaps even the voice, or the particular animation of that face carrying itself amid the sea of other faces.

And yet, after so many years swimming in the same pool, I no longer watch the bodies as much as I used to. Or not the bodies of people I know, or of swimmers I see there with some regularity. I see their bodies passing in the water, but like familiar signatures; they do not draw my curiosity in the same way as when they were completely unknown, when their mystery was most fertile. By the corresponding (if inverse) experience on dry land, do I therefore not look at familiar faces as much as when they were still unknown to me? But every face remains a mystery, even under cover of the familiar.

I SUPPOSE IT IS LIKE RIDING A BICYCLE (a generic way to talk about learning, or how the body and its reflexes learn; how many things taste like chicken?). Not swimming itself especially, for that can amount to little more than knowing how to not drown. Rather, beyond the splashing and thrashing, beating one's way through the water as if it were a blanket of nightmares one might struggle to throw off, I'm talking about endurance, reaching a steady measure of calm in the midst of one's exertions. After all, water is calm, and when it is not, we don't usually swim in it. More than that, a body of water at rest is irresistibly calm, it helps to calm us whether we are observers, or floating on top, or immersed in it (though not over our head). A bit of surface agitation—passing breezes, a few swimmers (short of a full swim team)—is as nothing, for the overall mode of a body of water, its natural state, is to be at rest. When I swim my laps, even though to some degree with my strokes I am cutting my way across the surface of the water, I feel something of its calm; with my long breaths I share in that calm. But it took a certain process, an apprenticeship, to build up to that state.

If, when I swim, my body is indeed on automatic pilot, who is that pilot and where did he learn to fly? That first winter and into the spring of my newfound discipline, I worked my way past a quarter-mile to a third, and three-eighths, and lo, half a mile. Pushing further to each greater increment, I would maintain that level a few days to acclimatize myself to the extended reach, to the larger span of time upon which I was launched. And then having grown comfortable with that more ambitious stretch, I would push on almost without effort. So that, with each added marker of time or distance, the sense of achievement diminished somewhat, and half a mile seemed only . . . half a mile. Swimming a kilometer, though, felt like I had broken onto another level entirely. That was, after all, a whole number.

Perhaps for the better, I also got to test my gains through translation into other numbers. Sometimes because of the hours or the particular day, I went instead to swim in the Jean Taris swimming pool (named after the Olympic swimmer; Jean Vigo made a film about him), which was closer to where I lived, a few blocks up the hill past the Place de la Contrescarpe. That was a more modern facility, a bit less character, smaller too, and with natural light only at one end. The pool was twenty-five meters in length, so it took sixty-four laps to swim a mile. Which posed its own advantages (greater play of ratios) and disadvantages (no exact thirds) in the game of numbers. But a kilometer was a nice even forty laps, and that really sounded like a lot. By the time I reached that distance, I could look back over the months and surely wonder how I got there.

Using the Jean Taris pool also helped prepare me for the next move. Not only was it the next big step in my aquatic development, that move was also geographical (temporary), biographical (return and extension of personal history), even a form of external and internal research. Along the way, I did attain the next small increment, to three-quarters of a mile (thirty-six or forty-eight depending, a bump up from thirty or forty respectively, the kilometer mark), but that was minor by then. In those years, living in Paris, I used to go visit the States about every year and a half. For the first time, in my new incarnation as a swimmer, I had an interest in taking advantage of a privilege offered by my parents. Ever since we moved to Berkeley at the beginning of the 1970s, they had had a membership to the health club facilities at the Claremont Hotel. A majestic old hotel, at the south end of the Berkeley hills, the Claremont had two outdoor pools: one just for laps (unheated; twenty-five yards long, or seventy-two laps to the mile), and a larger one that held several lap lanes but also kept nearly half the space open for general play (slightly heated; twenty-five meters long). Even now, I couldn't afford to belong to the Claremont club, between the cost of membership and annual dues, but I have greatly appreciated the privilege of going there as a guest over the years (and so have my wife and kids). I mean, this is California, easy weather most all year round, glimpses of palms and other trees when you lift your head out of the water, and clouds in the sky, and panoramic views of the bay before you get down in the pool; not the same as municipal pools, even in

Paris. I had it as a project, then, to work my way up to swimming a mile, while visiting my parents in Berkeley that spring.

It was also the right moment to push toward that next level. Dunking my head in an American pool—willingly, as an adult—seemed like a fitting frame for the occasion. And the fact that I did not have to contend with the ever-present possibility of random collisions in Paris pools helped facilitate my determination. Thus was I able to devote all my attention (my body's attention, if not always my mind's) to the pure pursuit of extending my endurance.

I LOST ALL INTEREST IN TEAM SPORTS around the time I entered adolescence. Maybe that has no bearing here, but I did not begin to appreciate, or to really notice, the social dimensions of swimming until well into my first year. An individual discipline, in which a sort of sensory isolation predominates, swimming posits its own system of planetary bodies, a constellation of separate forces, motions, purposes, with no center of gravity or burning sun. At the pool, we partake of a transitory society that is always changing and in which our silence is the mother tongue (or where speech is secondary, at best). But if we do not so much communicate directly, our interactions are nonetheless many.

It is these various interactions, far more than mere body language, that convey what might be perceived or instinctively constructed as personality among us. Not that this even has to be translated into words, but sometimes the result is a nickname by which I think of certain more or less regular swimmers. One example is The Blind Girl (relax, my wife uses the same moniker for this woman): even with her glasses on, coming or going in the vicinity of the building, she seems not to see me, after numerous times when our paths have crossed. But in the pool, she wears no goggles at all—how does she see where she's going, or does she? When someone first enters a lane where others are already swimming, there are certain basic rules of behavior that people may not always agree on but are common sense enough. If two people are splitting the lane, the new arrival should presumably make sure the others are aware that now they have to swim in circles. The Blind Girl doesn't bother, she just launches forth and the rest of us manage to avoid a collision with her. Further, there is usually the matter of assessing the pace and rhythm of the other lap swimmers already present and entering the flow of traffic accordingly, so that no one is crowded ahead or behind, at least as a starting point. The Blind Girl, on the other hand (maybe because she doesn't have her glasses on?), never seems to worry about such fine points; no sooner does she arrive, she slips into the water and casts off, heedless of her neighbors.

Something else is going on with another swimmer I know, a neighbor, who enters the group lane at a reasonable interval, but ploughs ahead with such drive that she inevitably gains on me. Once she has passed me a few laps further, however, she seems to slacken her pace, so that for a long while I must remain the same short distance behind her. At last, having controlled the game, as it were, she stops to switch over to another stroke.

Then there is the fellow I sometimes think of as The Fireman. Not sure quite why, maybe his robust build, maybe his straight-cut looks and trim moustache. He seems mild-mannered enough when he talks in the locker room. But in the pool, with his long frame, he leaves a wake no matter what stroke he employs, even while simply pushing a kickboard. I had long considered him nearly a lunk, for taking up quite a bit more space dynamically in the pool than seemed convenient to others. It was not always easy sharing a lane with him, though he did make an effort sometimes to mitigate that effect. Gradually, I warmed up to him a little, not at all for his swimming style but rather from scattered details I learned about him, mostly through overhearing: that he was older than I imagined, in his mid-60s, that he had first learned to swim at that pool as a child, that he had retired early and was now running a small charity group that sent materials to Africa. Thus, my idea of his oafishness had been softened by an appreciation of his human dimensions. And then came the day not too long ago when he had an altercation with my wife, who swims just a bit slower than me. I manage somehow to get along with all sorts of people in the pool, nary a conflict, I work around them, they work around me; not she. My wife is polite in that she pauses at the end to let faster swimmers get by, whereas The Fireman is one of those who stops periodically and then takes off again using a different stroke. He had stopped, she turned at the end to keep going, he started up again and soon overtook her, cutting her off at the other end. They had an argument about pool etiquette, she ended up screaming at him—and I caught none of it, because I had finished and was taking a shower. A couple days later, when I exchanged a few idle words with him as I was about to get in the pool, she came out of the locker room and grew enraged to see me chatting with the man who had insulted her and whom I evidently failed to defend her against. I do not know, in the end, what to make of the fellow, whether he's really brutish as charged or not quite. I am glad I have not seen him there much since then. I just want to go swim in the pool, not enter into any battles during that hour.

MORE THAN IN MOST SPORTS (another term I do not normally use for this activity), the accessories one might equip oneself with for swimming are fairly reduced. Or so I like to think (besides various accoutrements like flippers, I've even seen waterproof headphones—why get in the water, at that rate?). A bathing suit and goggles are about the minimum. All I add to that are cheap flip-flops, to protect my feet from the plantar warts I've occasionally gotten from the standing puddles on the way to the pool. Ah yes, a swim cap too, as if that helps protect my hair from churning in the chlorine.

Bathing suit: a basic Speedo. I seem to have taken it on faith early on that a minimal suit was most befitting to a serious approach to swimming—just keep the goods in place and carry on. In more recent years, people I know have been wearing close fitting shorts that go almost to the knee, but so far I resist. What seem totally not serious, though, are the boxer-type trunks, the loose sort that surfers wear. Not a chance, too much loose material.

The goggles are the real trick. In the past year, I've come to wonder if—though no mirror presents any evidence that I can see—my eyes have gradually shifted out of the normal balance. Maybe they've migrated to the same side of my nose, like in Picasso's portraits. Picasso eyes would explain why each pair of goggles start to leak barely a month after I bought them, so that they don't even make it six months before I've given up on them. I used to wear Speedo and other brands, then some years ago I discovered an Italian brand of goggles, Aqua Sphere, that were really an improvement: held their seal, didn't cloud up. About every ten or twelve months, I'd happily spring for a new pair, just over twenty dollars. But earlier this year, the last pair failed me. The lifeguard once told me I should be washing my goggles with soap, instead of just water, so I was doing that. But now he pointed out that it should be in cold water, because warm will stretch out the rubber. I'm such a dummy. Probably too late for that pair. But he also said they should be tightened equally on both sides, which hadn't occurred to me somehow, and of course mine were not. Still, that did not remedy things enough for my prematurely dying goggles. At last, after the summer, I went for a new brand entirely which he had enthused about, Blue Seventy. They were nice, reliable, and the solarized effect (the only model available) seemed to light up the pool. But not two months later, in the same left eye, water was leaking through again. Did Picasso not leave an antidote behind?

ONE OF THE GREAT METAPHYSICIANS OF TIME, Marcel Proust, wrote how some days are as though mountainous and we struggle to get through them, while others seem all downhill and we just fly along. Swimming too can be like that. There are days I'm convinced that my pace is slower than usual, I feel the effort more, whether because I didn't sleep as well, or I've been eating too much, or who knows. And yet I discover, when passing other swimmers whose pace I'm familiar with or afterwards glancing at the clock, that I did my mile in roughly the same forty minutes as always. The same in clock time perhaps, though not in my muscles and limbs, in the feeling of resistance offered by the water. But is the resistance itself ever any different? I suppose if a number of vigorous swimmers were all paddling away in there with me, it might require more effort to ply my own dogged path, or if the water temperature were markedly off from the norm. No, surely it is the feeling that varies, probably more than the external circumstances. And by the same token, there are days when I have the impression that my strokes are so robust–whether, again, from insufficient sleep which has cast a sharp edge to my energy, or some special determination, or even suppressed anger–I must really be cutting through the water as if the wind were at my back. Nor is that the case either, I find: forty minutes, give or take, remains indelibly my time.

ON THE MATTER OF RESISTANCE FROM THE MEDIUM: water contained in a pool is a measure to control the circumstances; not so, spread out in a pond or across the infinite body of the sea. We swim by seasons in these, and only where we can gain access. Ponds are easiest to swim, when big enough: the open space, and few if any to share it with. But the sea, that ancient vastness, all we touch is but the shallows.

When I swam in the sea, it was the Mediterranean, in Cadaqués, Spain (Catalunya). I used to go there in the years before I took up swimming and all I did in the water was get wet, swim around a bit maybe, and get out. That first year I was swimming seriously, I visited Cadaqués months after I had achieved a mile in swimming pools, and so without the fixed unit of laps, a certain quantity of which lasted a certain duration of time, the object was to fix on a chosen point in the distance across a stretch of the small bay and to swim there. This I did, uncertain of the actual measurable distance or how it might feel once I got far enough out, before I reach the other shore. In a sense, the shape of the coast there is ideal for such swimming: from the center of the village, with the mountain at your back, the land stretches out like two long arms encompassing the bay. But in fact the coastline is more sinuous than it appears at first, curving in and out, like a series of coves big and small, a scalloped coast. Some of those beaches offer a leisurely swim, while others present more of a challenge, depending where you start out and where you set your sights.

As usual in that period, on my more or less yearly visits I stayed with my Argentine friends Tomás and María, who rented a beautiful old house right on the water, with its own minuscule beach. Their house was located one and a half beaches from the center of town, shall we say, approximately to the south: the road from over the mountain comes in at the center of a long curving beach, upon which a number of cafés and even more restaurants and shops look out; facing the sea, if you follow the local road to your right around the sea wall to the next beach, Sa Cueta, and continue past that along the further stretch, as if walking into a famous early Dalí painting, and you reach that point and follow the road as it goes on to the right, where the houses block your view of the sea, just past a small alley between houses through which one glimpses the sea and which was always one of my favorite views, there one found their house. So, this was the time of challenge, my visit there in the late summer of '85. From the back patio, one could see another trick of the land, across a larger, not quite cove or bay, with the stretch of two nearly continuous beaches called Llane Gran and Llane Petit, beyond which following it around over rocks one reached a stone bridge (the water beneath was seldom more than ankle deep), and on the other side of that bridge was a *presqu'île*, an almost island, small and rocky, where a wide path led easily up to the top. The side of that island which was visible from the Llane Gran and Llane Petit beaches and also from the two-person beach behind Tomás and María's house, and further still even from the beach at Sa Cueta, was quite accessible scrambling down from the top over the low growth and also, I discovered, from the water where a gradual shelf full of mussels and algae and also sea urchins led to the shore. Sometimes at the near end of that side of the island, or at the far end, was a lone fisherman with line cast, and along one or two smooth clearings of bleached rock might be nude sunbathers. These details I must surely have noticed on previous visits to Cadaqués—though I had usually tried to avoid the busiest and overcrowded summer months—but that was all before I had become a creature of the water.

Well, I arrived that September now a swimmer, capable of going nonstop for a mile back and forth and back and forth in a pool, so what was I to do with the great Mediterranean Sea laid out softly before me? I had my jellies, for stepping over the rocks and all else at the bottom of those waters and which only weighed a little on my feet (counteracted by the buoyancy of the salt sea?), and I had my trusty goggles. So, the very first day after my arrival (about a 16-hour journey coming from Paris, what with the overnight train from the Gare d'Austerlitz, the local train from Port Bou to Figueres, and the bus over the mountain to Cadaqués, plus the waiting between connections, to set foot there past one in the afternoon), and after Tomás and María went off in the late morning to work in their boutiques, I carefully descended the stone steps to their tiny beach and walked out into the water. I was facing more or less toward the island, a little to the right, and I just started swimming to see how far I might go.

There were all these new elements to swimming in the sea, of which I had only the barest notion in advance, if at all (I'm talking about swimming for distance). For one thing, there was no stopping once you started. Sure, if I had to I could pause and tread water or just take it easy with the breast stroke, even glide along on my back and gaze up to the wide sky. But my purpose was to make a real effort with the crawl, and as much as possible I tried to maintain my usual pattern of breathing, lifting my head from the water on every third stroke. Somewhere along the way I had discovered, in swimming, that breathing on alternate sides kept me balanced and more prone to cleave a straight line through the water. That was my baseline for breathing, as it were, my normal pattern–because swimming is above all about breathing. From moment to moment conditions in the water may affect that, of course, and then you adjust, you breathe when you need to or else you simply have to have your head out of the water more often, in order to see what's around you. Even if, by late summer, the sea is supposed to be quite mild in temperature, once away from the shore I discovered that the water's depths rendered it, if not exactly cold, somewhat bracing, so that the first days I had to catch my breath a bit at the start of my swim, since my body, or specifically my chest and the whole breathing machine, had to get acclimatized to the vast grip of the sea. The process took some moments, which I was forced to recognize and accept in effect, before I could impose the force of my own breathing upon the water. The tone and temperature of the water were not, however, all that constituted the sea's embrace: like any living body it had its own movements, which I could speculate upon from the shore, assessing almost imperceptible breezes and the slight rise and fall of its surface, but once inside those movements I had to instinctively adapt the tenor of my own movement. Did I swim differently? Hard to say with any certainty. As I propelled myself forward over the variable undulations of the water's surface, my body rose and fell accordingly (as if I had a choice); while I was conscious of this added motion, like the gentle rocking of a cradle on an ever-swiveling axis, it did not particularly hinder my ability to keep swimming the crawl and to take a breath on every third stroke, though now and then it might throw a kink in my own smooth rhythms. But what posed the biggest obstacle to my simple enterprise was the human presence, in all its multiple intrusions. I suppose each instance might also be seen as a potential waystation in case of emergency, and in the back of my mind I considered that outlook, yet in practical terms it meant I always had to keep an eye out, when lifting my face from the water, for hazards near and far. Such hazards comprised both stationary and moving objects, though inevitably I was the only swimmer. The stationary obstacles were spread around over the first third or half of my trajectory from Tomás and María's little beach across to the island, a distance that I would guess to be at least half a mile (a kilometer perhaps?), and these were both small (buoys) and large (boats). The buoys could be tricky, from my angle of vision at the surface of the water; some were small enough that I might not see them until I was almost upon them, though I often spotted their chains underwater first, leading down to the anchor at the bottom. The boats ranged in size, even a dinghy, though nothing too obnoxious, and just about all had engines. Many had a small Catalan or other flag flying from the lines. Occasionally I might glimpse someone puttering about on deck, or a group having lunch or hanging out, but I never bothered to interrupt my swim to venture a greeting. At most, we would watch each other as I passed. In this way, my path could hardly be laid out in a straight line but rather a series of tacking segments around those boats and buoys, the cumulative effect of which was to reinforce that hypothetical straight line. Amid this random maritime parking lot, I also had to look out for boats that were moving—whether going out or coming in, they proceeded slowly enough at that point (usually), but from my swimmer's eye view it was not always easy to catch their movement, against the backdrop of stationary boats. Out in the open water I would spot them from some distance, and then it was a matter of assessing their speed and if they were likely to pass anywhere close to where I was going. Ah, but there was one more human element I had to watch out for that summer when I went swimming in the sea there, and the following summer as well when I came back, this one was capable of slicing me in half in the event of some unfortunate encounter and seemed like it could suddenly come out of anywhere. Windsurfers. I had no close calls, as it turned out, but often imagined the question raised by the sight of me swimming along for someone atop their board zipping past: What's he doing here in our playground, you can hardly see him! So, with all these obstacles in mind as I swam my stubborn path, I could not always insist on lifting my face out of the water on every third stroke. Sometimes I had to keep steady watch, and breathe on every second stroke. And sometimes for brief moments, I had to pause altogether and just look around, left, right, behind me, before I went on.

CURIOUSLY, EVEN THOUGH I SWIM FOR DISTANCE, as it were, the few times I went to the pool at Les Halles, it was not at all my favorite. At fifty meters long, Olympic-size, that meant the least amount of turns, of contact with the sides, and so by that measure alone the most like swimming across a stretch of the sea. But I would never want a pool to approximate the sea, why should it? (An amusing thought, perhaps—like Borges's map of the world that inevitably was the size of the world itself.) What is a pool without sides? And yet, fifty meters, that is a nice long stretch before you have to turn around and go back the way you came. I did have other reasons for my lack of fondness for that pool. It was too new and shiny (which did not mean necessarily that it was the cleanest, though you also had to step through a foot bath on the way out to the pool). And it was underground, with bright artificial lighting, which rendered the whole experience a little unearthly, like the video of a dream. What's more, it was located in the newest extension of the labyrinthine modern mall—most of it underground, though its central square was designed around a sunken opening outside, letting in natural light to the hub of its passageways—that was built in the 1970s on the site of what had been Paris' colorful and exuberant central market district (which I never got to see, having arrived in the city in the spring of 1980). The pool was about a block to the west of the main area of the mall, along an underground avenue that included other municipal offerings, most notably a well-stocked record library that seemed rather like a reward for attending to physical discipline.

Still, my slight antipathy toward that pool owed most to its size, I think, and the sterile seriousness it lent to the practice. Though some other Paris pools were marked off into lanes, at least in part, this place was all business. By the look of it, they really took that Olympic thing in earnest. Fortunately, not every swimmer there was a racing hound. But in that very fifty-meter length, contrary to its ultimate purpose for competitions, I felt a certain lack of tension in having the sides so far apart. From one end to the other, with the monotony of the unchanging tile floor, it was all so long that my thoughts seemed to wander too far, as if each time I would almost forget where I was by the time I reached the wall and had to make my turn. The sides, I understood, marked a kind of duration—the distance-time relation once again—which formed part of my own rhythm, where the movements of my body, and of course my breathing, found their proper phrasing.

THE VANITY OF FORM. Once, some years back, a woman who used to swim when I did suggested I pay more attention to getting my elbows up when lifting my arms out of the water. So, ever since, I have often been conscious to do just that. But other body parts have also stirred my recurring awareness, as I try to keep all the elements working in smooth, well-proportioned and synchronous movements. That is one advantage to maintaining a steady pace, rigorous yet unhurried. Others may sprint past me, I don't care: most often when I watch them pass, it is easy to see in their headlong rush the sloppy lurch, the lumbering commotion, the gangly and unsymmetrical clattering of limbs hauling the body forward any old way, the sooner the better. A quiet voice inside me shakes its head at yet another, hellbent and heedless, all fury and no form.

I have sometimes imagined, instead of the randy playboy or sex kitten and their specially outfitted bedroom, that it might be nice—or instructive, or amusing (or distracting)—to swim in a pool with a mirror along one side. Lacking that, other swimmers are my mirror. Or rather, seeing where their movements are wanting in harmony, or efficacy, or just proportions, I may better reflect on my own—even if I cannot see my body's movements, I can feel them in some probable approximation of how they really are. A particular point of focus is my legs: how many swimmers have I seen, fast or medium paced, whose legs trail like lost appendages, kicking well below the surface of the water, hardly in sync with each other, like two passengers who might or might not be riding on the same body? Every sighting of such travesties of form is another reminder for me, though my legs usually cooperate nicely even when I forget about them, as I often do. Maybe I'm lucky, in that respect. When I do think of them, I can feel my feet already kicking at the surface of the water, legs extended more or less straight and working like scissors. I can feel the air on my heels and the kind of turbulence my kicking causes there at the surface, which is different than in the thicker medium below. Where I have to pay attention, though—and here the mirror of others also helps—is sometimes, instead of my legs facing parallel to the bottom of the pool, they swivel a bit to left or right, according to the side on which I am lifting my head out for breath. I should be turning only my neck, the minimal gesture necessary for taking a breath.

Another point on form—though how it applies to my own swimming, and walking, I cannot know, short of extensive use of cameras or eyewitnesses—I've often noticed a substantial discrepancy between a swimmer's floppy or ungainly style (asymmetrical, at the very least), even what might be seen as the expression of a certain personality, and that same person's bearing when walking from the pool or to the locker room. All the more so once clothes have been put back on and the person is walking through the lobby or out on the street. This is certainly not always the case, but many times the difference is striking enough, in the smooth or unsmooth fluency of movement, through water and over the ground, that I am inclined to think our swimming is never entirely natural, in the way that our walking is; that whatever balance and symmetry and grace and economy we may achieve in our ability to move through water is due to a particular kind of learning, not as a result of becoming Homo erectus but in reaching toward another, possibly more ancient model, and doing so we contrive, as it were, a sort of borrowed form.

IMMERSION IN THE WATERY REALM, especially swimming in public or semi-public pools, bespeaks unseen elements. On one end of the chemical continuum is the human effluvia, spit and sweat (and we'll just leave it at that) cast off by the body in the course of our efforts. To counter that, to neutralize those individual contributions to the communal kitchen, the lifeguards or master chefs add some molecular seasonings to the stew. So that even accidents from the children's hour need not jeopardize our health. I don't recall ever taking chemistry even in high school; would I be swimming if I knew better? Chlorine seems to be that magic ingredient which allows us all to shove our faces, our bodies, into the large confined pool without having to share each other's microbes. In other words, it helps limit the damage of our collective intimacy. So, what is it about water and the conveyance of such effluvia that we might take in some trace of their possibly noxious effects, swimming in the soup? Do these elements, along with much else, dissipate far more easily in the open air we all breathe? What about freshwater ponds, and the great eternal sea, that we swim in? I know that the salt and iodine in sea water does something comparable to the chlorine in preserving us from the bacteria–though surely poisons, as from industrial chemicals and oil spills, are another matter. And dim as my grasp may be of these processes, it is worse when I try to make sense of how that works in the freshwater ponds I have swum in. Periodic rain water, decomposing plants at the bottom, not to mention occasional bird droppings (don't forget the fish) and once in a long while a dead cat or some other small creature: What makes it safe for me to swim in such bodies of water? Is sunlight really enough to complete the purification process?

Would I like someone to explain it all to me? Maybe not. But based on my experiences of different pools, I know that all applications of chlorine are not the same. I've read that private pools most often use a different chlorine compound, sodium hypochlorite (bleach!): could it possibly be softer on the skin as well as the breathing passages? I have to consider the atmospheric distinctions of places too, like hard water versus soft (even if I can never quite tell which is which) and the fact of what's simply in the air, or not, like the lack of humidity in California. Are the outdoor pools at the Claremont Hotel private, in these terms, and our regular pool at the Eastern Athletic club at Grand Army Plaza public? Point is, I recently swam five days in a row at the Claremont pool, with no sign of the symptoms that can assail me after such frequency at our local pool. Likewise, in my years of going to the Paris pools, two days in a row, or even a single day sometimes, could be enough to set off an allergic reaction that grew worse through the rest of the day: reddening eyes, runny nose, sneezing. The chlorine caused this, I'm sure, and the humidity of the city, variable by the day and the season, surely aggravated it. Twenty years ago, I underwent a treatment of allergy shots for several years, and ever since (so far) I seldom have such allergic reactions—except, sometimes, from swimming in the pool where we go, though the reactions are not as strong. And yet, at the 'private' pool, none of that: not the drying of the skin, especially around my eyes and lower legs (as if, with enough of that treatment, I might begin to resemble a piece of salt cod), nor the incipient drip, the wheeze and tickle in my nose.

At our local pool, there is another play of seen and unseen elements that I haven't noticed in other pools (vague memory of such from my Paris days). Some days the water is a little cloudy, occasionally the visibility is so poor it's like an underwater tulle fog that would cause collisions were it not for the restrictions on occupancy of the lanes; my first year in New York, I noticed this a bit in a couple of other pools (attributable to the water here? the people? the mix?). Usually the lifeguard gets the dosage just right and the pool water is more or less crystal clear. But dosage of what? Is this another property of the chlorine, or is there more to the formula of maintenance, another chemical to paddle through? Sometimes I even sort of like it, adds a dreamy touch, like an underwater film noir, swimming in the cloud.

WHY DO I DO THIS? What this? Swim. To get to the other side, of course. No: the other side, soon as I get there, becomes like where I started and I have to get to the other side again, so on and so forth forever more. Or maybe not, maybe there is an end to the infinite circle—predetermined usually. A function of limits on our time, or as a containment to our particular brand of madness. In which case, if there wasn't a pool, we wouldn't be mad? How else could that strain of madness be expressed? Not running around a track or even a path in the park. Mice do that. We're not mice and we're not runners (most of us). The breathing's not the same, the medium's not the same either. The monotony is of a different order. Or, some people find swimming monotonous, even swimmers; I don't.

But why stop at round numbers like a mile? Won't the body send out signals at the appropriate time? Swum out for the day, let's go. On the other hand, it could be seen as a kind of music. To immerse oneself in it for a while, as a regular thing. To recall our aquatic selves (and to put a numerical frame around the experience, as if to mark it off, to highlight it).

Sure, there are many ways to quantify the swimming. And none of that matters, really. What counts about the distance is—like dolphins, like sleepers—reaching that level of dream and having some time to dwell in it. The water residency. At least that's what counts for me. Maybe that's why I have always said that the hardest part (and thus the initial challenge) is getting wet. Making the transition, that whole intimate preparation for crossing over to the other materiality—not light and dark, we do that all the time—from air to water.

SWIMMING ACROSS THE BAY OF CADAQUÉS was certainly a challenge, and possibly—if I ran into trouble out in the middle of the water—a hare-brained idea too. That late summer of '85, a day or two after I first covered the trajectory between Tomás and María's beach and the little island, having just emerged again onto that island, I sat on a warm rock to take in the view. As a newly minted swimmer of distances and feeling my strength, what I saw was not merely a picturesque shoreline but temptation. There across the water, to the other side, did not look so very far: one could swim across it. But could I swim back? I didn't see why not; I felt in my body I could. The air was warm, the sea was calm. Why not? I knew I could do it. I guessed the distance all together—from Tomás and María's house to the island, to the other side of the bay, and back across to their house—was somewhere around two miles. With rests in between. It still seemed very doable (and I have never wanted a motorcycle, nor tried hang gliding nor anything flying through the air). My feet were a little as in space boots, weighted slightly by the jellies, but I was glad to have the protection as I stepped into the water over the encrusted rocks. When I was in almost to my waist, I pushed off out into the bay and set my course for straight across. Though I had rarely had much indication of it, having nearly always swum in pools, I knew I was good at swimming in a straight line. Whether that would be affected much by the movements of even a calm sea, I didn't know. My confidence in possessing the instinct for a certain linear rectitude was due to that simple balance I had achieved with the alternating of my breathing. In any case, there I was heading further and further away from the shore.

Slow but steady progress I made swimming across the water, my head facing down into the opaque green-blue depths. With nothing to expect for a long ways, I could even shut my eyes a short while as I settled into what might be called a rhythm of patience. But I didn't dare play for more than a long moment at being blind. Gently rocked by the sea's own light breathing I was able to maintain my sense of linear rectitude without much resistance–at least on that first day. I swam and I swam and I swam, and when I lifted my head to look around me, certainly I had advanced across the water but not so much, in the big picture. I was very far from the shore, though still not halfway. And the further I got, the more I had to keep an intermittent eye out for small boats coming and going and also for windsurfers. More than once we passed within waving distance of each other.

I don't imagine crossing the water took so terribly long, like going to the swimming pool or thereabouts, but in the time that I was piecing it out, one stroke after the next, with all its elemental nuances and small changes from moment to moment through sea and sky, that crossing seemed epic. And well before I had reached anywhere near midway across, I was certain I could do it. That may seem a little backwards but the way it works, I believe, is that you launch forth into your harebrained scheme not at all certain that you can do it. You think you can, and that's the best you've got going. But once you're in the flow of it, and you feel the effort, you know more surely. In the same way, some nine months later, I could tell when I was maybe a third of the way across that it was going to be a difficult crossing. Enough that I was so relieved when I finally reached the other side, I decided to walk back through town in nothing but my Speedo bathing suit (not that anybody cared) rather than swim back across through the slightly choppy waters, which put up more of a fight than what it seemed they would in the distance.

I was, of course, rather proud of my exploit when I saw Tomás and María at lunch time that day. But I was also relieved to have successfully risen to the challenge I posed for myself. Would it still be a challenge tomorrow? I felt certain that it always would be. There was something more I gathered from making that swim even once back and forth: an intimacy with the sea as though engraved into my skin, softly, as from long wearing. That was another reason I would go back there tomorrow and every day that I could.

ONE OF THE FRINGE BENEFITS IN GETTING MARRIED was that my wife's parents had a large pond. Out in the country (more or less, still), a large round pond. Back before we had kids, and when they were still small, we used to go out there more often. Much of that time I either had not yet found a convenient pool that I liked in New York or, once I went back to graduate school, was not going to the pool often enough and so let my gym membership expire. Therefore, whenever we took the bus out to New Jersey between May and September, I looked forward to swimming my now infrequent mile again in the pond.

Even if I could swim in a straight line, the trick here was to bend it a little into a constant arc. I was not about to change my habit of alternate side breathing, but lifting my head each time and glimpsing my general coordinates, I was able to adjust my path instinctively to skirt the largest circle possible, short of running aground in the muck of the shallows. And yet, I never quite understood: How does one swim in a circle? Is it a curve of the body, a way of leaning into the water, a slight emphasis in the stroke on the inward-turning side of the circle? The mechanics seem like nothing, almost, until I start to think about it. Shouldn't swimming in a circle be a more complicated affair than in a straight line back and forth between two points? What it comes down to, I think, may be as simple as the tension between the straight line (the swimmer's body and implicit movement) and the arc (round pond). And even removing all forward motion, figure a sleeper in a round bed, I still find a certain disconcerting incongruence.

In any event, away from a swimming pool, the old questions of distance and measurement remain. Once again, I'm compelled to guess by way of the time spent swimming (as if I had a watch with me) how many circuits (laps?) around the pond it takes me to swim a mile. As if it really matters at that point; but still, one wants to establish a point of reference. So, somehow I concluded that eight times around made a mile, approximately. Which was kind of nice, of course, swimming round and round in a sizeable pond. Away from that margin of the outer rim near the shallows, you couldn't see very much looking down into the water: a greenish fog, but with changing casts of light. Swimming by the outermost path, you could glance over the layered bed of leaves underwater (the pond was ringed all around by tall trees) and occasionally spot fish up to a foot long. When you lifted your face to breathe, there was the wide sky over you way above the trees. And even so, somehow eight times around could almost seem more monotonous than back and forth and back and forth in a pool. Strange, that. Like slow-motion sightseeing, only you're looking at different things when you're swimming around a pond. I guess it's another kind of zen in a pool, like you're on a grid so your mind is able to wander more.

Dutifully, though, for some years at least, I complied with the imperative to swim in the pond when conditions merited. Round and round the pond. For a good bit longer than anyone else stayed in. My head in the water off on my own. A pond, it seems, is a much more social setting than a pool, and yet there I was off on my own making up for the laps I didn't do in a pool. Long past anyone would want to wait for me–and that was nice too, for a while, the forgotten duck paddling around, nearly forgetting himself.

However, ringed by trees like that, the swimming hole was very, shall we say, biological, not to mention botanical; among other sediments carried by the air onto the surface of the water, through much of the swimming season there was also a fine dust of pollen that fell. In those first years circling the pond, I was fairly allergic to various sorts of weeds and things growing out in the country; so, despite the tranquil paddling round, a while after I had emerged sometimes the sneezing and itchy eyes began. From there, combined with old house mildew, the reaction just got worse through the rest of the day and night. By the next day, recovered and rested, I would plunge in again. After all, I didn't have my allergic reaction while I was actually in the water, bathed in its green coolness with no chemical additives or salt ("it's all rainwater"). And from the perspective of a swimmer, I couldn't not go in just because I might be sneezing later. I had the duty, in a way, to take advantage of any body of water that would have me.

LIGHT, IN WATER. Always a thrill to look under the lid, the lid of the water. Not that there is so very much to see, but that simple act, eyes behind goggles, dunking the head where it cannot naturally dwell for long, to behold anything at all underneath, is like a magic passage. So that, even before the barest of elements, one wants to see more, like a privilege that one does not easily relinquish. Even a pool in the dark would offer its own sprawling pages of light, a strange diffuse light perhaps, but with its own drama and mystery.

Certainly every place to swim, every body of water, offers a unique set of circumstances for underwater viewing. The pool at Eastern Athletic, seven floors up, windows around much of three sides, but particularly along the southern wall, gives to the morning sunlight ready access. Sunny days, whole columns of light cast into the water from angles both direct and oblique, careening off the tiled walls below, so that the glimmering reflections hang at one end or another like a diffuse curtain, swirls of ivy, a loose handful of jewels floating before my path. From one morning to the next it will differ, with the shifts of light and cloud, the angle of the season, the folds and transparency of the water. But on overcast days, there is plenty of light still, even if untraceable to a single source. The incessant crinkling of the water's surface, as of every depth, multiplies the mere presence of light, so that from one end to the other of the pool an endless script unfolds below. Not in any language but dazzlement, nothing to hold, no discernible shapes to reproduce, no start or finish. Like a phosphorescent algae, though without the algae; a writing, with no pen, that we pass through again and again, to no noticeable effect.

A wonder that we are not mesmerized by the play of light, that we don't swim into walls in our distraction, that we can keep to our straight lines. In ponds or the sea, by contrast, where all that dissolves settles to the muddy bottom, the light as well dissolves. Usually what we see depends on the depth of clarity, but the what is inevitably plants and fish and, still in the shallows, the very nature of the bottom as it sinks away. But sometimes I have managed to see the light itself as it plunges below in beams or sheets or endless ribbons. Out on the open water, it may be a friendly presence or it may blind us, it's all the same.

UNPLUGGED, DISCONNECTED, UNREACHABLE, unavailable, off the grid. The medium of water, so easy to enter—but like a door that shuts silently behind you, imperceptible. A particular kind of departure, personal and absolute in a way, solitary. When I am with my family somewhere and I go off swimming—even if they go swimming too, my wife nearby, perhaps even my daughter, while my son eagerly shares my lane or chooses to partake of a like trajectory—I am nonetheless in a realm of my own. Once I launch forth, my head immersed, all the more so in a pond or the sea where the sides are much further apart, no one can get through to me. My departure lasts as long as I choose and cannot be interrupted by others except through great effort. There is a certain magic in this act, as well as a kind of danger—almost within reach, in plain sight (if others are looking), and yet so far from things outside, walled off by the sound of water washing in my ears, that the world could have changed immeasurably while I was "away." In this regard, just as there is always the chance we might not come back any time we depart, I almost feel like I should say goodbye when I go off to swim. Will you still be there? Will I? But let's not get carried away.

AT LEAST TWICE HAVE I SWUM OUT to the middle of the water and discovered that prevailing conditions were a little rougher than I had anticipated, such that I felt the need to calm myself, don't panic, keep swimming and you'll get where you're going. Where was I ever going? The other side? Only to come back again. The most worrisome time occurred in Cadaqués, crossing the bay the summer after I'd first done it. I'm pretty sure this was not the first such excursion during that visit, so perhaps I launched forth with too much confidence about my elements-defying abilities. Besides, I had already traversed one leg of my triangular trajectory, the short side–from Tomás and María's little beach (or maybe even from the beach at Sa Cueta, further back) to the almost island–so that I was able to better gauge from in the water, rather than standing on the shore, the heft of the wind, the heave of the swells. But while I could feel the sea was acting up a bit more than in previous days, it still did not seem overly agitated–so I thought from swimming that first stretch of my trajectory, which was closer to the shore and thus more sheltered. From the rocky shore of the island gazing out across the open bay, I saw no whitecaps, no noticeable peaks and valleys in the swells, so I plunged forth to continue my familiar route. Not till I approached midway in my crossing–three-quarters of a mile across, did I say?–did I realize how much resistance I was struggling against (and not my own, for once). The wind (more than a light breeze, at any rate), the shifting ridges on the water's surface, as I got out into the middle of the bay, confounded my advance. By the time I grew conscious of the contest I was in, nowhere near any moored or passing boats, it seemed an equal wager whether I should go back or push on. The forces mounted against me were hardly uniform in their direction; there was no path of least resistance, by which I could coast and preserve my strength; the agitation of the sea was just enough to make for a test of wills. I remained certain (more or less) that I had the strength, so with no choice but to endure, I kept to my slow, methodical pace, determined to advance.

Where else could I go? The strong embrace of the sea was not an unpleasant feeling, though it compelled me to direct my thoughts, along with my body, forward. I imagined the lunch crowd in the open air restaurants oblivious to that invisible speck in the distance, that meshuggeneh way out there battling what to them would appear a calm sea. I imagined my friends on shore going about their daily business, or lying out in the sun for an hour, and if the question of my whereabouts crossed their minds, it fluttered past unanswered, unimportant, oh he's somewhere. But was I even somewhere? No way to set a place marker, or draw a line to trace my path. In the sea, for a mere human body, all location gets folded under, shuffled about, dissolved. At times, when it seemed I was hardly advancing (while convincing myself of an incremental, if imperceptible, progress), I also had the impression of finding myself in one of those compact personal swimming pools where the wave motion is mechanically generated to the desired level of resistance, and you swim and swim, never going anywhere. A compact personal pool stretched out to the size of the sea. Only how, in such pools, do you swim out into the middle? Can you overcome the resistance to get that far, or can you modulate it somehow while in the water? And most importantly, do you ever reach the other end?

What would it be like if the sea began to gain the upper hand, would there be warning signs? My arms growing weary, snag and pitch of breath. I was still managing to breathe on every third stroke, and if a swell caught me unexpectedly in the face, I would breathe on every other stroke for a while. At such moments when the sea increased its challenge, or even beginning my swim on days where the water seemed just enough colder (due to a change in the wind or the weather) as to make difficult catching my breath at all, that was the means—taking a breath on every other stroke—by which I eased into the greater stability of breathing on every third. But even the fact that I was able to think beyond my immediate efforts, to people on shore or far away (everyone was far away just then), meant that I hadn't reached a critical stage yet, right? Unless, of course, I was already delirious. At some point, I had indeed passed more than halfway across—though I still had so far to go it was necessary to take up the breast stroke for a few moments, in order to reassure myself by way of all possible visual references. What was happening with time, I kept wondering, how long is this taking me? As long as I kept up my strength, it didn't matter really. Was I hungry yet? I thought I might be, but it was hard to think of food exactly. All the same, I tried: more reliable and accessible than other pleasures, it served (minimally, at least) to help drive me forward by sheer projection. Grilled sardines at Casa Anita; paella at Sarrita's; ah, the grilled rabbit with aioli at Casa Nun, yes, I could almost smell it. Not that I imagined a sumptuous platter might await me there the moment I stepped out onto dry land, but the wavering images may have greased the engine a little. Or was it merely a form of lifting weights for the imagination? My powers of concentration were hardly optimal just then.

Nonetheless, the diversions occupied me long enough that when I glanced again, I was somewhere around two-thirds of the way across. No question anymore that I would reach the other side; and though no one was waiting for me exactly, anyone who knew me there or elsewhere would have no reason to think—on my account anyway—that it was other than a normal day. And it was a normal day, of course: a day in which someone surrounded by water contemplates the possibility that he might drown; a day in which, somewhere else, others do drown; and where no particular reason would lead anyone on shore to think, even for a moment, of who will or won't come back.

A similar thought occurred to me some twenty years later, on one of our visits to Deer Isle in Maine. The day after we arrived, I think, at any rate it was late afternoon and the overcast sky was threatening to pour forth, but still I or we wanted to swim. So I drove a mile down the road to Long Pond, where I had swum every day for a week the year before. How dangerous could it be to go in a pond, even a big one? When you can see all the sides, what harm can there be? I think my wife or my son had come with me, but they turned back, the water felt cold. Again, it was not until I'd been swimming a while, half the length of the pond, that I became aware of struggling against a kind of current whipped up by a wind that had seemed less than negligible before I plunged in. Now it seemed I was hardly advancing, out there in the middle of the water, and no one cognizant of my efforts. The current on the pond was not just pushing me back, but to the side as well sometimes; if I was stubborn and determined enough to continue my swim along the path I had intended, for a certain interval that appeared to be possibly at the risk of my own survival. So I persisted, and when I turned around at last at the far end—where there was nowhere to climb out—I could only hope that the changeable winds would turn round on me as well. And yet, in the midst of my struggles, lifting my head out of the water to glance around me, it was so peaceful along the shores where not a single person lingered.

SOMETIMES WHEN I AM LEFT ALONE in my swim, whether in a pool or a pond, and I do not have to keep conscious of other swimmers around me, I'm moving along and I start to wonder: where is my mind drifting off to? Here, for a change, it has free reign to go where it will, my mind has a mind of its own, and I am ready to follow it, like a curious observer. And then I notice, it's not going anywhere. Nothing; no wandering; no wayward thoughts at all. Except for the primary mind wondering, pulling one curtain after the next, to find only emptiness. That's good, I think, that's even very good. Isn't that also the object, to empty the mind, while the body runs its engines? But it's like trying to fall asleep: here I am lying in bed waiting for sleep to take me, except that I'm thinking I'm still not asleep, maybe I should stop thinking, how does one do that, empty the mind; but there are sounds in the room, and outside, and I hear my own quiet breathing; an itch, let it go, don't scratch, but if I don't, I'll keep thinking about it; either way, my thoughts flit about, in no hurry at all to be gone. And once I stop thinking about them, of course, they're gone. So, either that's when I fall asleep or, since I'm actually swimming, they start to wander, my thoughts, like dreams, free associating. By the time I catch up with them again, I'm more than a little surprised at the banal and unexpected byways they've traversed. And no sooner do I apprehend a fleeting thought, see where it's going, it darts away once more.

THE EGO OF SPEED; of perceived speed. As in so many other respects, I have usually seen myself in terms of the tortoise rather than the hare, steady and slow. Except I am not slow in the pool; nor fast either. I'm medium fast, as I've said, with no concern for going any faster. And I refuse to let others pressure me on that account. The first year I lived in New York, over twenty years ago, I tried the Carmine Street pool a couple times. Very busy, the water constantly churning, was my first impression. Still, I found room in a group lane and so I set forth. Swimmers who are notably faster, I always figure, can pass me with no problem and most often that works fine. But this happened to be a time when one hot shot didn't like that sort of implied arrangement–the lane may have been too busy for him to pass easily each time, and maybe I didn't stop enough at the turns for him to pass (the super hot shots will pass me every four to six laps, but most don't)–and somewhere about a half-mile along he stops to tell me quickly at the turn that I should be in the slow lane. Now, that's a tricky thing to say to a fellow swimmer. In effect, he's declaring to me that I have no clue about my own abilities, my own relative and proper place among other swimmers, and that I should in fact be demoted. It's all the more dispiriting to realize, in that quick instant in the midst of my swim, that the fellow is wrong but it doesn't matter: I either go in the slow lane, where I will likely have it worse than this schmuck does (precisely because I will be too fast for the majority of slow swimmers, and thus an annoyance to them in turn, which will of course be frustrating to me as well), or I stay where I am and continue to deal with the hot shot who thinks he has more right to be there than I do. Either way, the pleasure of swimming has vanished completely–and certainly in group lanes it is often compromised, in that body and mind have to contend constantly with the pace of other swimmers, since almost no one goes at the exact same pace as another. As I recall, I continued in that lane where I was, but left before my mile was done. However, the experience reinforced my initial impression of the pool as being too busy for my tastes, and evidently too much of the shark eat shark world that typifies New York (or, Manhattan?) at its worst. At any rate, there is that choice on entering a public pool marked off with such lanes. How do I assess my own abilities, especially when confronted with the swimmers who are already there? I imagine that, like me, most swimmers are neither irredeemably slow nor former competitive swimmers. Prevailing conditions aside, some measure of self-image mixes in with an honest self-assessment, and presumably one does the best one can. All the more so to realize that such prevailing conditions are constantly changing, according to the mix of swimmers in a lane and even the tenor of those in the solo lanes. Add to that swimmers who change their stroke every so often, for a mixed workout (I really dislike that term "workout," especially for swimming—not my concept at all). Thus, the shifting polyrhythms, the variable pace that seems to dominate in different zones of the pool—different time zones, as it were, different time signatures. So, it turns out that all sense of speed is endlessly relative—and the ego that goes with it, merely another illusion.

That would be the lesson for those of us who normally go in the fast lane, but who sometimes due to circumstances swim in the slow lane of the pool. We swim at our normal speed, but when we pass other swimmers too often the notion of speed becomes especially meaningless. What is the pace of our passing? We are aware of swimming in a place that is not properly ours, and if we find ourselves too far out of sync with those sharing the lane we become an obstacle to each other. That is what the methods of organizing a swimming pool are meant to avoid.

AS A DISTANCE SWIMMER (I'm sure that for real distance swimmers a mile is barely serious, a minimum at best), I have tended to think of visual distances in terms of whether I can swim them. Across the Hudson River? At the right place to do so, sure, why not. The English Channel? I might be up for it, in the appropriate conditions. But beyond the temptation and imagination's ready leap, such grand crossings are doubtful, I realize, if only for the public risk involved. At least in America, the public must apparently be protected from itself (only on some fronts, obviously), or its own hare-brained recklessness will decimate the population. Thus, not only am I safe from the sudden urges of my own thoughts, but we may also be comforted to figure that any nut with a wild idea to jump in and swim across–to wherever–cannot simply go ahead and do so. He must first pay some kind of admission. Then, if he's going to paddle furiously out into the middle before realizing that he has not the strength to go anywhere now except down, at least his fee will help pay for any authorities that might be available to assist.

Still, it's a persistent fantasy for many of us swimmers to imagine ourselves in any sizeable body of water that we may pass, or glimpse, or else read about on a roadside or in a newspaper. Even spotting a little lake on the GPS as I drive up the New York State Thruway, that blue finger hidden from the road yet nearby, my thoughts cast about for an entrance while I am already that lone figure calmly plying the waters, the flash of my wet elbows working like steady pistons, my body itself almost invisible on the surface gliding forth. And going where? The end, though in sight perhaps, remains indistinct. Why did the chicken cross the road? The other side didn't matter, it was all in the crossing.

But chickens don't swim, regardless of my reverie. And I understand that somehow, like a figure cast by a magic lantern onto a blank wall, the phantom swimmer does not appear in a flock or a pair but alone. All alone. Swimming is not inherently a social sport (for those who look at it as a sport—I don't); at most, in a race, everyone is against everybody else. Like running, it is about the singular body pushing at its own particular limits in a specific medium (if we had wings, would we also be flying laps?). So, the idea of a marathon does not, to put it mildly, appeal to me. As in, a big group of people—a crowd—participating in the same singular activity alongside each other. Sure, the company of others helps to spur one on (unless, of course, a whole bunch of chickens are crossing the road: inevitably, some will just turn about in confusion—why am I doing this? where are we going? if a chicken can think in the first person pronoun—until at last the car crests the hill to come put an end to their conundrum); and I do not question the silent benefits of company. After all, doing something a little crazy—like swimming the English Channel?—seems much less so when done surrounded by others doing the same thing. But then, no less true is another angle on that: the crowd permits, gives access to, certain kinds of crazy, which no individual is likely to step aside and question.

Marathons are about distance and duration, and consequently endurance, and usually presume a group engagement. For all sorts of practical reasons, as well as financial and legal connivances, most distance challenges for swimmers are only possible as marathons. That is, such challenges tend to be projected onto very public spaces, so special cooperation is required to enable the event, which by implication becomes a public event; any personal component is subsumed by that condition. Hypothetically, though perhaps not legally, I could step into the Hudson somewhere and swim across, but no one is going to alert boat traffic of my personal whim (roadside warning: Chicken Crossing) and no one is going to watch out for me in the shifting currents. But the other day I received a group email from a friend at the pool, fundraising for a swim he'll be doing next month, among many contestants, as a benefit for River Pool in Beacon. I'd read about the event before, and thought it tempting: entry fee of $50, must raise at least $100, start across the river and arrive at Beacon, about one mile, with a party after. Not too expensive, I might do it one year or another—only chance I'm likely to have to do such a swim. And yet, from my own perspective on the discipline, it would be a departure: certainly I can imagine swimming with the pack while focusing with a zenlike insistence on the continuous rhythms of my own physical practice, but in the end I would manage in my way to be part of the festive group on the other side. However, even to entertain that possibility is to reinforce my general antipathy to the approach overall.

My thoughts on swimming marathons were already reignited a week before my friend's email when an article appeared in the Sunday edition of the *New York Times*, on the front of the Metropolitan section, about open-water swims. On the second page was a list of half a dozen swim events in the area between July and September. The highlight of the article was the 8 Bridges Hudson River Swim, covering 120 miles down the river to the Verrazano Bridge over seven days. The writer claims that 900 such events, more than ever, will be held this year in waterways across the United States, including the sold-out swim around the island of Manhattan, for a fee of $1,775. Who pays that kind of money? Of course, the fees benefit various causes, as well as the sponsoring groups, after covering the costs of boat crews and other support staff. Of the other marathon swims listed, I like particularly the course between Battery Park, at the tip of Manhattan, to Sandy Hook, NJ (17.5 miles)–no temptation there, simply it tickles me to think that all it takes is a swimmer in the water to connect the two points. But overall the whole apparatus of these marathons–from the fee to the pack of people to the public event–turns me off. As a predominantly interior practice (obviously I have my own particular perspective), it doesn't seem right to make such a spectacle of swimming.

A CURIOUS THING, going to the same pool with a certain regularity. Even on a first visit you strike up conversations, but going back again at the same time and making that a habit you cross paths, make eye contact with what become familiar faces. Sooner or later words are exchanged—no hot water; the slobs who leave their towels on the floor—and months or even years after, names are offered. You get all kinds of details—you give out all kinds of details too—triggered by a t-shirt, the temperature of the pool, waiting for a lane. Some people surprise you by what they tell, but when you're standing there with all or most of your clothes off, particularly in the locker room where nakedness is the common coin, it seems natural to reveal a certain amount of personal matters.

During a rare instance when I bothered to wait for a lane, the older woman who came to sit beside me and whose face was somewhat familiar, explained why she always waited for a solo lane. Beyond the simple preference for swimming alone, she revealed that for some years now she only had one lung—I think she lost the other to cancer. I was impressed she would tell me so much (plus a further complication, as I recall), but it served to soften the gruff exterior—and I let her go ahead of me to the next free lane.

Too many times I have heard myself recount stories of my bicoastal upbringing, my years in Paris, my kids and their schooling—all quite normal, people tell what they have, what they've lived. But at times I have wondered: Didn't I tell these same details to someone else here recently? Is there somebody in the next bay of lockers at this moment thinking, Doesn't that guy talk about anything else? And yet, with a certain continuity the stories develop. One guy I often see at the pool or after in the locker room, when I say hello, how you doing, he invariably replies drily, Still married. But I've also learned many other details about him, gradually: that he has three kids, the youngest, a son, slightly older than my daughter, now in college; he's a few years older than me, is an Orthodox Jew, works in real estate (owns a few buildings, I think), and has a place upstate where he often goes for long weekends and which is beside a lake or large pond where he swims regularly; that his oldest kid, a girl probably not yet thirty, lives in Israel and is one of those Orthodox Jews who intends to have as many children as she can, she's now up to five; also, that he's a Republican, so we rarely venture anywhere near politics—because we seem to like each other. Another fellow I know from the pool, likewise for over a decade—he still gets my name wrong occasionally, whereas the other guy and I have never exchanged names directly though we know each other's names by way of other people referring to us—often tells off-color jokes in the locker room, usually sexual and typically male-oriented, sometimes embarrassing of course, though often funny. And then he'll happen to change his spots to tell a funny one (or three) that couldn't be more chaste. But over the years I have also heard about his two marriages, his several girlfriends, his desire to be more sexually active than any one of these women seem to want, and thus the logic for seeing two or three women at a time on different days; also, the latest, his decision to get back together with his second wife, the Jewish one—he's from an Italian family, raised Roman Catholic, and thus tells priest and nun jokes too. The girlfriends of the last few years are too crazy, he says, and need his help too much, even if they were kind of exciting at first. In his early sixties, he was once a high school teacher and then became a lawyer. He also has two grown kids, by that wife, and a house in the Caribbean that he rents out.

Have I heard too much about his life, perhaps? I don't think so, though I've certainly heard a generous portion. Another fascinating fellow whom I haven't seen at the pool much the last few years, but whenever we run into each other on the street near the gym, or in the locker room, or upstairs by the weights, he tells me volumes about his upbringing in a small Puerto Rican coastal town, notable figures in Nuyorican culture he used to know (such as Pedro Pietri), his frequent dealings especially in real estate with Chinese and Orthodox Jewish businessmen, such that he has been treated as family, the ballroom dancing classes he attends, his two sons who served as military specialists in Iraq and Afghanistan and have at last retired. He's ten years older than me, moved to New York with his family as a teenager, and the fact is he always has more stories and commentaries, told with a smile. I would like to hear more about his travels throughout Latin America back in the Allende years, and much else, so each time I linger long enough as to miss some of my swim time or to arrive almost too late to my car (alternate side parking rules–I have gotten a few tickets leaving the gym too late).

There are days, in other words, where the interior expeditions of swimming are almost eclipsed by the unending discovery of other lives, other journeys, set aspark by the continuing dialogue with familiar faces.

FAR AS I HAVE OBSERVED, watching others swim, considering my own practice—the rhythm of my stroke, how I push off at the turn—there seems to be no discernible inclination toward a lefthandedness in swimming. Or righthandedness either, for that matter. Should that be surprising? I don't know. We don't think of lefty or righty runners; though when the arm swings an object (even a fist) or the foot kicks a ball, there the preference certainly does enter. Is that because in swimming and running both sides—and both halves of the brain?—must act as equal partners?

Of course, I might not be the best test case. I am mostly right-handed, but not entirely. I have always written with my right hand; but, at the table, I have always cut my food with my left hand, fork in the right. As a kid playing baseball, I threw the ball with my right, glove on my left—and yet, eventually I came to be almost more comfortable throwing with my left. Thinking about this again yesterday as I swam, I noticed that I tended to reach for the wall at the end of the lap with my left hand. And then, pushing off again into the next lap, when taking my first breath, I would lift my head out to the right. And so?

It may well be that many swimmers, when swimming laps free style and if breathing on every other stroke (ie. always on the same side), do show a preference for the side on which they perform other tasks (writing, etc.). In breathing on every third stroke while swimming laps, on alternate sides—a practice I adopted consciously early on in my swimming life, and I have no idea if it is predominant among regular swimmers, though I suppose so—I wonder if that is a way of maintaining and even restoring a certain balance. I can easily imagine it might have greater implications for the body and all that is percolating inside: alternate-side breathing, while swimming, could serve as an ongoing realignment of the left and right sides—the limbs, the spine, the brain.

LIKE ANY LONGTIME SWIMMER, I have swum in many pools and each poses its challenges as well as pleasures. In that summer, the first year of reaching a mile as my regular measure, I had been going to the Paris pools almost daily and so when I went to my friend's film festival in Avignon for a week in July, I missed that newly acquired habit. One evening, a screening was held at an outdoor club–maybe it wasn't a club, but the screen was set up at one end of a large patio that served as a social space for recreation, in the middle of which was a modest pool. Since he told me beforehand that there was a pool, I brought my suit and goggles. We arrived early, still an hour of daylight–and I no longer remember the film. There wasn't anything else I had to do, and no particular desire to socialize, so I put on my swimming briefs and got in the water. Of course, I was the only one. I was in sunny Provence, it was summer, perfect weather–why wouldn't I swim? The pool was long and narrow in its proportions, but actually not very long for a lap swimmer; the kind of pool not really meant for a serious swim, but big enough for a casual splash and then some. There were not a lot of folks sitting around along the sides when I first got in, so if I had been inclined to be self-conscious about my plunge, there was not so much audience. Problem was, the pool was just twenty meters long, if memory serves. It may have been even shorter, but that sounds about right. Fifty laps for a kilometer, eighty for a mile. The effect is, though, when the pool is shorter, you cover a certain stretch in pushing off, basking in that initial glide, and before you know it you're at the other end already. Pushing off here, pushing off there, back and forth–with such frequent turns, swimming laps may seem a bit frenetic. Or at least I was conscious of that appearance, whether or not anyone bothered to notice. At the same time, that didn't stop me from getting in my laps, I was determined, back and forth, back and forth again and again. It was glorious, in its way, in the Provençal light, which gradually I grew aware was declining. I also began to perceive, when I lifted my head out for breath or at the turns, that the seats and cushions in the vicinity of the pool were filling with more people. The anticipation of dusk, and with it the film, was palpable, like the chatter of birds at that hour in a village square. Stubborn, I kept on and reached my eighty laps, quite satisfied with myself, of course, for having taken that singular opportunity. When I finally stopped and stood at one end to take off my goggles, no one seemed to pay me any mind—like a creature doing what it does, over there, and now perhaps no longer. Nor was I embarrassed, getting out, all wet and mostly naked except for my swim suit, as I went inside to get changed.

WHAT DO YOU HEAR WHILE SWIMMING? One might well consider each of the senses in such circumstances, for swimming is a kind of obstacle condition where the normal operation of the different senses is blocked or altered, even subverted. As when one is blind, say, and the other senses bend and compensate and take over some of the territory that was left unthinkingly to sight. Water is our darkness instead–if that analogy is not already excessive–which suggests that, if such was our primordial state, the senses we practically take for granted once served us in other ways. We might equally ask: What *can* we hear, with our faces in the water? How does sound reach us, and which sounds?

Always the sloshing in the ears, our heads carried forth in a perpetual wash cycle. It's amazing how quickly these sounds rinse out from the resonant bowl of our skulls, as soon as we stand up out of the water. But other sounds come through too, depending where we are swimming. First, inescapable, there is the sound of our own breathing–not so much when we inhale, it turns out, catching the air in our mouths directly from the sky; rather, it is the action of the air pushing out from nose or mouth in a channel through the water, that much we hear. At the Eastern Athletic pool, there is not so much else in the immediate vicinity except the accumulated splashing of other swimmers. Although, once in a while, there is this to penetrate even the most oblivious ears: a loud siren, some say from the sauna for some reason, yet each time I think of it as a fire drill. Swimming my laps, as the siren goes on for a couple minutes, I keep watch to see who will stop and get out, until I'm the only one left swimming (how is the fire going to reach me in the water? what will it feed on along the tiled sides?), except no one does stop, we all ignore it (and since when are fire drills held for grownups?). Still, I'm amused by the thought of us all parading outside in our swimsuits, as though our real identities would thus be revealed.

At other pools, though, other spots to swim, a different resonance holds, and so a distinct sonic recipe may reach my ears while my head is immersed. Outside, like at the Claremont, where people lounge about in row upon row around the pools, I might imagine splinters of conversations that fly off unpredictably in my direction while I swim, but the fact is the voices would have to be quite close by—standing about in the next lane? it happens—for me to hear them. Instead, without a roof overhead, birdsong and the faint roar of jet planes filter through when I tilt my ear out, along with a particularly strident voice or even the lifeguard's whistle calling the kids to order. Above all, it is the ambient sound that is different, swimming at an outdoor pool, the sound itself has more space and dimension, compared to the box that contains us inside—swimmer, pool, and all. Further outside, as it were, in a pond or the sea, even more—sonically—drops through the air to me with my head in the water. The wind through the trees; the swing and drop, out from the shore, of a body off a rope; gull cries; the snap of a lanyard against a mast; the low chug of an outboard motor on the small boats coming in; the slight folds of the sea swell rubbing against each other, water upon water.

But especially in indoor pools, I realize, it is the sound of my own movement through the water I hear, and the sound of others' movement nearby, to each body and each stroke its particular contours, its sound/waves. Because when I push off the side, the water flapping against my ears sounds differently, of course, than in the middle of a lap, and differently still at the beginning or end of my swim when, head submerged, I am at rest: as is the water, sounding almost hollow, no body at all.

DESOLATE POOLS I HAVE KNOWN. I suppose it might have to do with the seasons–autumn, winter–and the location as well, out by the edge of the city. Stubborn in my practice, learning to be obsessive about it, in that first year or two of regular swimming–as if that almost daily regularity were an anchor, a measure, to which I might affix the loose order in the rest of my life at the time. Fleetingly single again, with a career hardly defined by external parameters, for me swimming surely marked a need for a certain discipline; it even provided the excuse sometimes–since I had no kids yet or family commitments–to absent myself from where I was (or simply to take a break from writing, or the attempt to write).

In that initial period, I met a woman and we soon began to see each other in what became a weekly pattern of 24-hour dates, from late Saturday afternoon to late in the day on Sunday, since she did have a job at a newspaper. I used to go to her place, take the 63 bus almost its entire route from the Rue des Ecoles to deep in the 16th arrondissement where she lived in a grand *deux-pièces* as befitted the neighborhood. As autumn turned to winter and we kept on with this opulent pattern, sometimes I brought my swimsuit and goggles and went off to the local pool, while she tended to other tasks. The first time, a light and early snow was in the air as I made my way past the Soviet embassy to the nearest municipal pool, almost at the outskirts of the city. Two or three people were doing laps when I got in, we steered clear of each other. With the attendant and the person at the front window who took my entry fee, that didn't make very many of us there. Was there also a lifeguard? Probably–off to the side, biding his time. The high windows gave a glimpse of trees outside and the gray sky. Under the fluorescent lights we clung to the surety of the water, as if we were the ribs of the place, laid out lengthwise, quiet shuttle to the weave. Built perhaps in the '60s, the whole interior seemed unearthly, with no possibility of welcome. But once I plunged my face into the water, I was in another world–as were we all, each an asteroid in our own orbit.

More desolate still, through the half dozen times I went there, was the pool way up in the 17th arrondissement, in the northwest corner of the city, a block or two from the *périphérique*. The cold and gray and inclement weather of the winter streets didn't help. But what is it about the edges of a city, the lack of definition to that zone which abuts the city limit, as if the city had already given up, no longer identifiable, indistinct? We had moved into a little house owned by friends of hers, well past the métro stop at La Fourche, beyond the Place de Clichy. The house was on a long narrow street, hidden behind a small apartment building in front. With a bit of a garden that one crossed in ten or fifteen paces, which received but scant direct sunlight, it was quaint and cozy for a couple first moving in together. But the proportions were not right, nothing that we owned fit well on those floors, and the extent to which we did not fit well with each other grew ever more apparent in the few months we lasted. All the more reason to remember: a man still has to swim, wherever he may be. If the little house seemed like a sort of exile from the city in which it was nonetheless located, so much more were those streets that I forced myself along to reach the pool. Merchants, pedestrians, we were all foreigners in that liminal zone, any one of us might have said to another, "You, too? And what brings you to this forsaken place?" Yet the pool–more sterile in atmosphere than the one at the edge of the 16th, with less in the way of windows, and its 1970s architecture still more impersonal–stood somehow as the refuge I needed after that trajectory. With even fewer denizens, I had only to submerge myself in the water and push off, to find my place.

"WATER ISN'T WET; it only makes you wet." How many times did I hear that from other kids when I was growing up? Is it true–or is it rather a smartypants distinction? "Covered or soaked with a liquid, such as water": that's the first definition of *wet* in my American Heritage Dictionary. So maybe those kids were right. Could water be "covered or soaked with" water? What is inside the water that would get soaked? Does it matter? When we speak of the qualities of water, in fact, the subject tends to escape us. After noting the obvious, that it is liquid, we only manage to speak like chemists or poets, or sometimes like physicists and engineers when considering its dynamic properties. The swimmer, of course, knows all these aspects from inside–wherever that inside is.

Water *is* its particular qualities, in a particular place at a particular time. In a particular body of water. We might even say it is the particles themselves we are looking at in that water, which make it hard or soft, clear or murky, fresh or foul smelling, calm or turbulent–as if the water were an essence we can only approach by way of its particular conditions. We swim in *that* water, we drink *that* water (usually not the same). As swimmers, we do have our limits, and each limit poses challenges which we might, wisely or foolishly, choose to take up. So, the water is also a kind of screen or stage, a liquid screen or stage, in which we project or play out our own personal drama. Is that what swimming laps is–not a discipline, not an exercise, not a sport, but rather rehearsals for a play that will never have its premiere (I'm not talking of you competitive folks who swim to race)? Further still from water in its essential qualities as water, and even from the particles and particularities, we are inclined to see water more in terms of quantity: the size of the body, the depths and distances it contains.

Water, it seems, is a medium–for transport, for reverie, for nourishment, for getting wet. If, on a molecular level, water retains a certain memory of what was diluted there–whether in a controlled environment, as for homeopathic ends, or in the reckless and ruinous expanses of so many ecological poisonings—it also carries a measure of our own memory, both collective and individual. So much water inside our bodies, and so we swim in bodies of water. By getting wet we are joined to all the other bodies that came before and are with us still.

also by Jason Weiss

Always in Trouble: An Oral History of ESP-Disk',
the Most Outrageous Record Label in America (2012)
The Lights of Home:
A Century of Latin American Writers in Paris (2003)
Writing at Risk: Interviews in Paris with Uncommon Writers (1991)

as editor

Steve Lacy: Conversations (2006)
Back in No Time: The Brion Gysin Reader (2001)

as translator

Silvina Ocampo, selected poems (2015)
Marcel Cohen, *Mirrors* (1998)
Luisa Futoransky, *The Duration of the Voyage: selected poems* (1997)